CLEV

IN OLD PH GRAPHS

CLEVEDON

IN OLD PHOTOGRAPHS

COLLECTED BY

JANE S. LILLY

Alan Sutton Publishing Limited
Phoenix Mill · Far Thrupp · Stroud · Gloucestershire

First Published 1990

British Library Cataloguing in Publication Data

Lilly, Jane S.
Clevedon in old photographs.
1. Avon, History
I. Title
942.85

ISBN 0-86299-696-1

DEDICATION: This book is dedicated to the special people I miss every day: Mum, Dad, Harry, Vera, Joyce and Maureen. And to my husband, Roger, together with the family and friends who keep me sane and the ones who drive me insane; they know which they are.

Typeset in 9/10 Korinna.
Typesetting and origination by
Alan Sutton Publishing Limited.
Printed in Great Britain by
The Guernsey Press Co. Ltd
Guernsey, Channel Islands

CONTENTS

INTRODUCTION

Having lived in Clevedon all my life, I have found it an exacting experience to have to judge what photographs will and will not be interesting to newcomers and locals alike. I hope I have made a choice which gives a balanced view of the town, neither too intimate nor too general. My aim in this introduction is to fill in the gaps in the picture of Clevedon's development as a resort, which cannot be demonstrated merely by old photographs.

All the Victorian guidebooks on Clevedon give the same romantically erroneous impression: that it was a small fishing village. There was fishing in the town; a survey made for Elizabeth Wake in 1630 details a fishery cottage, now 93 Old Church Road, but in the 1841 census, Thomas Lilly was the only fisherman listed. He continued to run the fishery as well as launching himself into the bathing-machine business in the 1860s.

This pattern of local people gradually combining their traditional occupations with new ones as the town expanded persisted throughout Clevedon's early development. Masons bought building plots and their wives took charge of the running of the lodging-houses they built there. Once some of the new houses were sold, young people whose only chance of employment previously had been to work on the farms were able to apply for a range of domestic work as scullery-maids, boot-boys, ostlers, coachmen, cooks, gardeners and house-keepers. So the locals were swift to benefit from the people moving into town.

But why did Clevedon expand so suddenly? The tendency is to think that there was nothing here before 1800; indeed, there was nothing to draw vast numbers of newcomers unless they wanted to invest in agriculture. The days of agricultural growth were largely past. The seaside boom had begun and, importantly, Clevedon was conveniently near Bristol. When Julia Miles was writing to William Barnes, the Dorset poet, on a tour of the area in 1825, she wrote, 'Cleavedon... just now becoming a resort for the gentry, we went to the seaside near a mile from Cleavedon where we took dinner and tea at an Inn lately built in the rocks.' At this time the beach and the seashore were still effectively a mile from Clevedon, because the area north of Old Church Road, the Triangle and Old Street had not been developed at all. The town consisted of cottages and farmhouses strung out along the last-mentioned roads, Kenn Road, Strode Road, Court Lane and the Moors.

The village had expanded very little since the survey of 1630 listed the 79 houses and cottages then standing. By 1822, when the Greenwood brothers wrote in their guide that Clevedon had 103 inhabited houses, where 107 families lived, 89 of whom were engaged in agriculture, only 24 new house sites had been established in just under 200 years. Those were mainly built in the final twenty-five years of the two centuries, after the 1799 Clevedon Enclosure Act was passed.

The Enclosure Act was really, I think, the beginning of the period of growth in Clevedon. Once the manorial wasteland was identified, the Elton family, together with their estate agent, began to sell small parcels of land for building, at first in a modest way. Local people began to buy land along the edges of the steep slopes, useless for cultivation.

The side of Walton Road against Strawberry Hill was one of the first portions to be built on. Richard Long had part of the old estate there called Chaffins and built cottages for himself and his brother and sister. Richard Hole built four or five small cottages, and also had land and a farm off Court Lane for himself. Cottages were built on waste ground between Old Street and the river, where the Health Centre stands now, and yet more went up in Old Church Road, between the road and the river, in front of Hangstone, the common quarry, near Salthouse Fields, and at West End.

The initial reason for this spurt seems to have been pressure of numbers on existing housing. But it inspired the Eltons and their estate agent, William Hollyman, to begin development in earnest in the 1820s, in a far more organized fashion.

In 1823 Hollyman bought a piece of land at East Clevedon Triangle and built Ilex Cottage and Trellis Cottage with its adjoining shop. In December 1824 a strip of land of seventeen acres, running from the beginning of Wellington Terrace to near the Little Harp, was divided into building plots to be sold. A new coach road was to be made from Clevedon to the sea; this followed the line of Old Street, Chapel Hill, Hill Road and, later, Highdale Road to the area that was to become the Beach.

William Hollyman realized that he was in an ideal position to take advantage of building opportunities. He had both money and imagination and, more importantly, good taste. His houses at East Clevedon were very elegant, Ilex and Trellis Cottages being followed by The Grove in 1827 and Rose Cottage 1 and 2 in 1837. He secured the prime sites at what was to be the junction of Wellington Terrace and Hill Road and built the Royal Hotel, Nightingale Villa and Champion House in Hill Road in 1826, jointly with George Newton. In Wellington Terrace, he built Wellington House, Cliff House, Neptune House and Cambrian House in the later 1820s, followed by more in the years afterwards.

His family was hardly less active in seizing the chance of involvement. Thomas Hollyman built the Rock House, Clevedon's first tea room, below the present Royal Pier Hotel, and ran a butcher's shop at Copse Vale House in Copse Road. Phoebe Hollyman was the landlady at the Old Inn in Walton Road, at that time called the Clevedon Inn because there was no other.

On a smaller scale, he was followed by many local masons, carpenters and tilers, who took the opportunity of investing their hard-earned cash. Fifteen years after the first building plots went up for sale, the majority of the houses in Hill Road, the Beach and Highdale Road were completed. This rapid growth was carefully controlled by the Eltons, who specified in the title deeds of each plot that the houses built on their land had to have had a particular amount of money spent on them, had to be fronted with freestone, or Roman cement in imitation of it and roofed with the best Bangor slate. No noxious trades were to be carried on therein.

On the Beach, the plots ran back to the edge of what was to become Copse Road. These plots were large enough to accommodate second houses, usually smaller, facing inland. The first four cottages in Copse Road are examples of this secondary development, and not, as is often claimed, fishermen's cottages. Because Copse Road runs between two fields, however, the opposite side was built later than the side behind the Beach, the second field being on lease as farmland until the mid-1850s.

Hill Road was developed at first along its north side, where all the plots had magnificent views of the Mendips and the Welsh coast to the south and west. Building began at each end and worked its way towards the middle, where the last plots were closer against the cliff of land behind. The same happened in Highdale Road, where the rocky central section was eventually blasted out. The East Clevedon Triangle end, locally called Coombe Hill, has several large houses built in the 1830s, but there are more at the Christ Church end, where access was from Hill Road.

With the arrival of the Bristol and Exeter Railway in 1847, some of the emphasis shifted from the newly-developed Hill to the Triangle, where the station was situated. Within two years, the Clock Tower pub, then called the Railway Arms, and Triangle House were built on the site of Walker's Farm. The shops built along the south of Old Street extended round the corner into the Triangle and towards Kenn Road during the later 1850s. The fountain now standing at the junction of Old Church Road and Victoria Road was erected in the Triangle in 1867, to improve its appearance for the benefit of railway passengers. Every decade saw more pairs and rows of new shops in Old Church Road, and the whole centre of the old village experienced a revitalization and boom in building.

Alongside this increase in building, of course, came necessary improvements in services. The first parish school opened on the site of Holdland House in Old Street in 1834, and was enlarged and rebuilt in 1858. St Andrew's Infant School followed in 1846, Chapel Hill in 1849, All Saints' in 1860 and St John's in 1879.

After the initiation of educational improvements came the realization that something would have to be done about a clean and efficient water supply and correct drainage. The houses in the old village had always taken their water from the rivers and ditches, and disposed of their sewage by the same route. The earliest houses are along the foot of the hill because the rock of the hill is limestone, which cracks and cannot hold surface water. Without the sophistication to build water tanks supplied from the rainwater collected by roof guttering, the farmers stuck to building on the clay lowlands beside a ready water supply.

In 1852 a sanitation inspector made a report regarding Clevedon which was so far from satisfactory that a Local Board of Health had to be established to make drastic and far-reaching improvements. In 1894 it became an Urban District Council but, in its forty-two years, had seen the emergence of the Water Company, the Gas Company, the police force, the Market Hall in Alexandra Road, the public weighbridge in Old Church Road, the Cottage Hospital and the pier.

One of the functions of the Local Board was to approve plans for new housing. Although records are sketchy for the years leading up to 1870, we know that they approved the building of houses in Albert Road, Bellevue Road, Chapel Hill, Copse Road, Elton Road, Linden Road, Park Road, Victoria Road and the later part of Wellington Terrace before that year. Development following 1870 included middle-class housing centred around Sunnyside Road, Princes Road, St John's Road and Avenue, Queen's Road and Madeira Road. This was the era of the workingmen's terraces in Kenn Road, Old Church Road, Meadow Road, Strode Road and Old Street. As Linda Murray points out in her thesis on Clevedon and its

Victorian houses, the bigger and more expensive the house, the higher up the hill it was built.

Naturally, with all the extra people moving into Clevedon, shopkeepers had to look to their laurels. In 1830 there was a shop at Byegones in East Clevedon Triangle, a butcher's shop by the Salvation Army Hall, a shop which used to adjoin Ashley House in Old Street, and serving the newer part of the town, the shop which is now Mark's the Chemist in Hill Road.

This situation changed very rapidly. Almost all of the shops on the north side of Hill Road are built over the gardens of the small villas and town houses which now stand half-hidden behind them. On the south side of the road are all of the purpose-built two-storey Victorian shops which went up from the 1850s onwards. The Triangle kept pace with this and, indeed, with the railway as incentive, developed even faster. Clevedon had two shopping centres quite soon after building started.

One of the things that separated the two parts of the town was difficulty of access for carriage traffic. The main way through the village for traffic had always been via Walton Road, Old Street and Kenn Road. The visitors and inhabitants who wanted to reach the newer part of Clevedon had to go along Highdale Road and Hill Road. Once they had got to the Beach, down the old part of Marine Hill (now the footpath from St Anthony's School to opposite the pier), they could loop round into Copse Road to get back into Hill Road and return the way they had come. There was a carriageway down Chapel Hill, but it was very steep. In fact, one of the reasons for the building of Christ Church in 1838/9 was that St Andrew's was so very inaccessible for traffic from the Hill. To a great extent the cutting of Elton Road in 1853 ameliorated this problem, making Old Church Road a main access route for both parts of the town.

As the town grew, so its religious needs had to be catered for. Christ Church was the first new church to be built for hundreds of years, but was followed by All Saints' in 1860, St John's in 1878 and St Peter's in 1898. The Nonconformists had been meeting in a cottage in All Saints' Lane until they built their Independent Chapel in Chapel Hill in 1827, opposite the Bristol Hotel. This was replaced in 1856 by the Congregational Chapel in Hill Road, opposite the top of Bellevue Road. Copse Road chapel was erected in 1851 by the Baptists, who put up their next chapel in Station Road in 1903. The Methodists built their chapel in Lower Linden Road in 1883, after meeting in Hope Cottage at 79 Old Church Road for some years. The Society of Friends built their meeting house in Albert Road in 1868, and in 1883 the Royal Hotel was purchased by the Franciscan Order, a church being added to the building in 1886.

St Andrew's church, at the western extremity of Old Church Road, is by far the oldest building in the town, dating back to the twelfth century. The next oldest building is Clevedon Court, built around 1320, and having its own chapel of St Peter. These two buildings, which in any normal village would be next to each other, are $2\frac{1}{4}$ miles apart here in Clevedon.

The suggestion is that the Augustine Canons, who had the right to appoint vicars here, had the church built near the sea because one of their missions was to save sailors from drowning, and that the tower was used for a beacon fire in foul weather. The Court is at the other end of the parish because the land in between was so wet and badly drained it was the most sensible place to build a manor house so as to have guaranteed access to Bristol over the hill at the back of the Court.

Highdale Farm lies in the centre of the parish, between Highdale Avenue and Highdale Road. The name has been corrupted over the years from Hidehall, a hidehall being the house from where the steward administered the estate. It is believed that the farm dates back to Domesday times. There was a chantry chapel at this farm, which the villagers could attend when flooding cut off the Old Church, as St Andrew's is called. Written records for the site date back to 1297, and clerics were appointed there until 1380. The Survey of Chantries made in 1548 discovered that there had been no priest there for some years, and that the land was let to farm. The house was rebuilt in the latter part of the seventeenth century, having fallen derelict.

During the same period a new technique in farming made its appearance. Instead of land being permanently meadow, pasture or arable, it became the practice of richer farmers to go into what was called 'up and down' farming. Several farms would be amalgamated, and over a period of years the land would be improved to the point where it could be ploughed and cropped one year, and grazed the next, then ploughed again, and so on.

This meant that investment in agriculture became very worthwhile, since after the period of improvement the yield from the land trebled. So it is interesting to see, from the collection of leases dating from this time, that Bristol merchants were taking up leases on as many as four Clevedon farms at a time. A lot of the larger farmhouses, though, fell into disuse and dereliction through this practice, since by letting the roof fall in, the lessee could avoid a proportion of the rent. Highdale was derelict at this time, as was Dowlais Farm in Strode Road, Tutton Farm on Yeo Moor, Whitehouse Farm and Stamfords on the Kenn Yeo, among many others. Some of these were rebuilt, some lost altogether.

One of the few farmhouses which has never become derelict or been rebuilt is Village Farm, now 136–8 Old Street. Next to Clevedon Court and St Andrew's church, this modest house is the oldest building in Clevedon. It is a yeoman's hall house, built around 1500, when it would have had a central fireplace on the floor, the smoke finding its way out through the thatch. There was one large room in which the occupants lived, ate, cooked and slept.

It is hard to imagine that the people who lived in Clevedon three or four hundred years ago lived in a village with tucking mills for cloth, a cornmill on the sea-wall, a rabbit warren which covered most of Dial Hill, the Old Park, a deer park and dovecotes. Lead mining was carried out for a short time on Court Hill and Dial Hill. Sheep were stolen, wine was washed up from ships wrecked in the Channel and you could eat the fish caught there without being poisoned. There were saltpans on Salthouse Fields. Even 150 years ago, the town was largely self-sufficient, making everything for its inhabitants from bricks to boots, in however small a way.

The motorway has brought more visitors, and more building. Twenty-five years ago, the population was around 11,000. Since then it has doubled. It is my hope that newcomers and locals alike will enjoy the book, seeing what Clevedon was and still is: the Village and the Hill, Old Clevedon and New Clevedon, inextricably entwined.

SECTION ONE

Setting the Scene

THE GARDEN AT THE BACK OF CLEVEDON COURT, depicted by Edwin Hazell. The terraces to the north of the Court are believed to have been made during the eighteenth century, following earlier defensive embankments. Gertrude Jekyll condemned the over-fussy layout of small, square beds here, though.

ST ANDREW'S CHURCH, photographed by Edwin H. Hazell before the extension of the cemetery and the addition of the current wooden roof over the gateway to the main churchyard.

A VIEW FROM ABOVE BATTERY COTTAGES AT WEST END. The new houses on Tennyson Avenue show beyond and to the right of Tennyson House, but there is no sign as yet of St Andrew's Drive, and plenty of fields in the distance.

ANOTHER PRINT FROM MR HAZELL'S GLASS NEGATIVES, this time taken before some of the bungalows filled in the gaps between the Victorian houses in Old Church Road. Apart from Hallam Hall on the crest of Dial Hill, top left, there is very little showing on Dial Hill Road.

THE BATHING MACHINES PROMOTE PEAR'S SOAP, an example of something used to popularize something else. The house to the left is the Pottery, shown before its conservatory was added. This is the Beach before front gardens had to be turned into car parking areas.

CLEVEDON ONCE HAD A SECOND TREE LEANING AWAY FROM THE WIND, towards the far end of the Beach, in addition to the famous one on the Green Beach. This was taken before the pathway was made below the road from the Beach to the Green Beach. Spray Point had not been built on the corner opposite the tree, and there are Barlow rails, curved ready to become parts of the pier, lying on the shingle. This photograph was taken in 1868.

THE BEACH from another angle in 1868, before Alexandra Road came through. There was only a footway behind the bollard. There have been many changes in the houses: the first is now a cafe; the third is the Moon and Sixpence; the fourth, the Pottery without its bay windows or the conservatory – a row of quiet lodging houses and private schools.

THE BEACH as we know it is wider than in this picture. This was taken before the extension of the footway towards the sea on pillars at the pier end of the promenade. The two white pillars behind the bathing machine housed a pair of davits, with which the larger boats were raised and lowered onto the beach. The house furthest to the right is Oaklands, now replaced by several blocks of flats.

THE PIER BEACH, with the old Spray Point building when Alonzo Dawes ran his Beach Auction Mart there. As he was manager of the waterworks, the waterworks office was there too. The buildings have gone now, replaced by maisonettes which blend exceptionally well with the Regency houses on the rest of the Beach.

YOU CAN SEE HERE why they needed to add windshields to the bandstand. The trees in the enclosure, now cleared away, show the wind direction very clearly. The walk round the seaward side of these trees was always called the Monkey Rack locally, a nickname for the first row at the cinema.

THE GREEN BEACH at its elegant best. This was always one of Clevedon's special features, and one of the Elton family's best gifts to the town.

BATHING MACHINES ON THE LONG BEACH. These were pulled beyond the range of the tide when not in use. There were complicated by-laws about ladies bathing on the Long Beach and gentlemen bathing on the Pier Beach. The gentlemen had to wear drawers or a waistband when bathing at particular times of day. It was, of course, taken for granted that the ladies would be fully covered anyway!

A CROWDED DAY AT THE MARINE LAKE, showing the triple-decker diving stage clearly.

COPSE ROAD. This was taken very near the turn of the century as the houses on the left had not been built in 1897, and the builder's scaffolding is just intruding on the picture. The wide, square arch is the entry to I.G. Stuckey's livery stables, now converted to mews houses. The canopy is over Ernest Shaw's butcher's shop, and there is the milkman bringing his handcart down the hill to the right.

COPSE ROAD from the opposite end. The cottages on the right are often said to be fishermen's cottages, but were in fact built in the late 1820s, when the Beach was developed. The enormous house dominating the end of the road is Lewesfell in Elton Road, run at the time of this photograph as a private school by Mr Joyner.

FRIARS PATH goes from Wellington Terrace up the back of the Friary, formerly the Royal Hotel. The building in the distance is the Edgarley, but the one to the left of the path may be one of the old garden buildings of the hotel, perhaps a gazebo. These were very popular in the gardens on the north of Hill Road, because of the Mendip and sea views.

A VIEW FROM BEHIND THE COTTAGES on the Zig-Zag behind Hill Road, built about 150 years ago by Thomas Poole. He called them the Lookout Cottages, and you can certainly see why. The view today is still worth the steep climb.

THE WALTON ROAD, with its row of cottages opposite the Old Inn, was on the line of the main route through Clevedon.

THE FIRST PART OF THE WALTON ROAD and a better view of the cottages, mainly built in the early nineteenth century when wasteland was sold for development. In 1830 the nearest was occupied by the Hayman family. Next to them was John Phillips, the cooper at the Old Inn.

THIS IS THE VIEW ONE USED TO BE ABLE TO SEE from the edge of Strawberry Hill by Bennett's Ripple. This predates the Light Railway, looking across to a handful of cottages without even the hint of any bungalows. The house almost in the centre, with the twin gables is Swiss Vale, a Regency house where in the 1850s Miss Gage established a 'Select Seminary for Young Ladies'.

THIS VIEW OF SWISS VALLEY from almost the same point in the late 1920s shows the Light Railway line very clearly. My aunt remembers travelling along this stretch when the driver and the fireman stopped the train and reversed it to see who had been correct in identifying a bird they had seen.

A VIEW OF SWISS VALLEY from above Holly Lane, looking southwards. Look just to the right of the Walton Road and you can see the line of the old Weston, Clevedon and Portishead Light Railway curving round the back of the little cluster of houses.

A FEW HOUSES ARE STILL MISSING at the top of The Croft, and the Light Railway trackbed can still be seen crossing Walton Road. The Croft was named for the field it was built on, Matthew's Croft. The cottages on the nearer side of Walton Road were in Walton, the ones on the opposite side, built by the Andrews family a couple of hundred years ago, in Clevedon.

THESE TWO COTTAGES IN NORTON'S WOOD LANE were owned by the Hedges family, who had owned an estate in this area since 1598. The one on the right was let to William House in 1857 with a quarry for blue Pennant paving and block stone, now Conygar quarry. The piece of land it stood on was called The Crate.

'THE WALTON ESTATE is beautifully situate at the extreme end of Wellington Terrace, and bids fair in a short time to form a fashionable neighbourhood,' said the *Clevedon Mercury* in 1867. It has certainly done this, from the nucleus of only twelve houses which stood there then.

SECTION TWO

A Few Commemorative Buildings

THE BEST PICTURE OF THE VANISHED SIXWAYS CLOCK that I have come across. It was erected to commemorate the coronation of Edward VII, but dismantled for scrap metal during the last war. Legend has it that it never kept good time.

THE CLOCK and Caple's Pacific Stores at the top of Alexandra Road, with sunblind in use at 12.30. The gentleman pushing the Bath chair was a professional. His invoice for one lady is said to have read, 'For a-pushing and a-shoving of 'er. . .'

THE CLEVEDON PRINTING COMPANY OFFICES beyond the clock tower. There are a couple of billboards for the *Clevedon Mercury* leaning on the wall, which has since been taken down. The horses and carriages along Albert Road may be coming from the Albert Mews livery stable there.

SNOW COVERS SIXWAYS, before the shops at the bottom of Bellevue Road were built, and before Mr Christie moved his dental surgery from Linden Lodge behind the clock. Linden Lodge was demolished to make way for the post office building.

STEPHENS ENGINEERING AND MOTOR CAR WORKS shows its old stone archway clearly to the right, where the carpet shop is now. The arch led to the back of the premises and the workshops; at the front Mrs Stephens ran her refreshment rooms for thirsty travellers from the railway. To the left is Newbury Place, built in the early 1870s, where G.W. Stuckey had a printing and bookbinding business. Beyond the clock is the cottage demolished to make way for Robinson's Café, now the Gas Showrooms.

THE TRIANGLE, again full of horse-drawn traffic. As my uncle says, the danger in crossing the road in those days was that you might step in something, not in getting run over. The curving row of shops behind the clock was built on the site of Rose Cottage, a small late-Georgian house. In 1897 you could have bought cough sweets there from Llewelyn's, liquorice from Mr Dike, borrowed some books from Emily Hockaday, or had some boots made by Mary Harris.

A BUSY SCENE, looking down to the old Great Western Railway station in the centre. The entrance at that end of the station was later blocked up when an embankment was made behind the buffers to stop the trains flying out through the end of the buildings! There was still a balcony on the shop to the left, as well as shop-fronts along Lloyds Bank's building.

THE TRIANGLE at the turn of the century, when the horse brakes still ran. Mr Probert was still running his grocery business in Providence Place, now the offices of C.J. Hole. My aunt remembers when the Bedminster factory women used to come down in a horse brake, once ending up in the ditch on the way home due to excessive entertainment in the pubs.

A PEACE MEMORIAL, not a war memorial, commemorating the dead of the South African Wars. Behind the three figures in the foreground, struggling against the bracing wind, is the stand for the donkeys to shelter in.

THE PROCESSION ALONG OLD STREET for the dedication of the Calvary in Walton Road in 1917 as a peace memorial. The Calvary itself is tucked away on the left side of Walton Road, just before the steep turn off for Strawberry Hill.

SECTION THREE

The Rich Man in his Castle, the Poor Man at his Gate

ORIGINALLY FRANKFORT HALL, then Clevedon Hall and now St Brandon's School, this is one of the outstanding houses in the town. In 1853 *Chilcott's Guide* had this to say '. . . a fine open coach road, connecting the old village with the Beach, its sides studded with elegant villa residences, especially one new building for C.W. Finzel, Esq., which is in a very commanding situation, and surrounded with large pleasure grounds.'

CLEVEDON HALL from almost the same angle in May 1897.

ST BRANDON'S SCHOOL when it was Clevedon Hall. These carriages arrived for the wedding of Miss Gertrude Hill to Major Ross on 5 August 1897.

THE GROUNDS OF THE HOUSE were of great beauty. Here is the Japanese pond, with the gardener standing at ease behind the latest thing in horse-drawn lawn mowers beyond.

THE POND was large enough to go boating on, in a small way.

GERTRUDE HILL, SEATED, AND MISS GOOCH, taking the air.

WICKHAM HOUSE, IN SUNNYSIDE ROAD, halfway through its demolition in the '70s. Wickham Court flats replaced it.

VICTORIA HOUSE IN HILL ROAD. Next door, to the left, is Simla Lodge, a house some fifteen to twenty years older, which it resembles quite closely. The stone carving on Simla Lodge is well worth a look, having different plants at the top of each stone pillar.

THE STABLE BLOCK AT CLAREMONT VILLA in Highdale Road. The main house was bought in the 1830s by a well-known collector of antiquities, G.W. Braikenridge. He brought back many items of interest from the Continent, and the fireplace which surrounds the window under the gable here, was one of them.

THE GROVE IN WALTON ROAD, opposite the Old Inn, a house seldom seen. This gem was built by William Hollyman in 1827, and retains its wine-cellars, butler's pantry, marble Regency-Egyptian fireplaces and a very beautiful oval domed skylight over the stair well. The original shutters, used to avoid harmful sunlight penetrating the house too far, are shown.

THIS IS ALWAYS CALLED GOLDING'S COTTAGE, after the family who lived there for many years. It is No. 70 Old Church Road, opposite Hangstone Quarry, and was part of the property of Thomas Young in 1830. Here, around 1900, you can see that nothing had been built to the south of it at all.

THE INTERIOR OF THE COTTAGE looked like this about eighty years ago.

THIS, THE SMALLEST COTTAGE IN HACK'S NEST, as this group was called in the Sanitation Report of 1852, has recently been completely rebuilt.

STAN NEWTON, the projectionist at the Curzon lived here. It was then No. 93 Old Church Road, but is now No. 139. The cluster of cottages was built by the Hack family between 1820 and 1850. Some have been totally rebuilt, but this one has just been extended. I regret the passing of the little clover-leaf windows.

THIS WAS TAKEN before the renovation of these cottages at Hack's Nest, in Old Church Road. Jacob Hack had built one cottage by 1830, and completed six more by 1839. The central one was a beer-house in the 1860s.

THESE COTTAGES have made way for Grove Pet and Garden Centre in Parnell Road. They were the subject of much debate for the Local Board of Health when they were built; the owner had the privies backing onto the river, causing offence and much reference to by-laws.

THE SCHOOL IN THE BACKGROUND ON THE RIGHT indicates that this is Miss Counsell's cottage, where the Job Centre stands in Old Street. The house was built around 1810 by George Newton. He also built a cottage fronting the pavement to the left of this one, but that was replaced many years ago by Clevedon Domestics' premises.

THATCH COTTAGE used to be the very last house in Kenn Road, and Mrs Griffin was a customer of my grandfather, T.H. Lilly, on his grocery and paraffin round. Here she is by the van in the twenties. There was a ladder on the van to reach goods carried on the roof.

SECTION FOUR

Refreshment

A GOOD SHOT OF THE OLD INN IN THE WALTON ROAD before the tall bay window projecting on to the pavement was removed. This is the oldest pub in the town, originally being known as the Clevedon Inn. In the days when horse-drawn coaches used to call here, the view from the bay would have provided a useful advance warning to landlord, ostlers and barmen to be ready for action.

THE WAGON AND HORSES before it was rebuilt in about 1905. The first landlord was Peter Moxham, who moved here from the New Inn in Old Street.

SALTHOUSE in 1905, when it was a private house. Victorian guide books say it was converted from two cottages used by the salt-panners. Salt was panned on Salthouse field from the late seventeenth century, by evaporation from shallow depressions into which the seawater had been allowed to run.

THE ROCK HOUSE was set so low in the rocks at the head of the Pier that it gained itself a nickname, as a remark in a letter of 1825 shows. 'We went to the seaside near a mile from Cleavedon where we took dinner and tea at an Inn lately built in the rocks it is call'd the Shippaground it is the most romantic situation I ever beheld.' It was run, almost inevitably, by those great Clevedon entrepreneurs, the Hollymans.

THIS VIEW INLAND FROM THE PIER, taken about fifty years ago, shows the remains of the old Rock House, below and to the left of the Pier Hotel. This gives more of an idea why the early nickname for the Rock House was the Ship Aground.

THE TOWERS was built in 1863, when it was sold along with six house plots to be called Atlantic Terrace. The road was later renamed Leagrove Road. Under Mr Oram's management, the restaurant could seat 400 for hot and cold luncheons, fruit and cream teas and salmon teas.

THE CLIFFE HOTEL was originally another of the large private houses built on Wellington Terrace for letting in apartments by William Hollyman. In 1963, when this photograph was taken, terms were from 7½ to 9½ guineas.

CLEVEDON'S FIRST HOTEL, THE ROYAL, built in 1826 was another Hollyman edifice. There were 11 superior upper rooms, 4 large parlours, drawing room, 2 kitchens, underground wine and beer cellars, coach house, 4-stalled stables and $1\frac{1}{2}$ acres of garden.

THE HYDRO, more recently the Edgarley, but originally the first of the houses built in Wellington Terrace by William Hollyman, and called Wellington House. The house became a hotel and was demolished in the last ten to fifteen years. The front door was taken to be used in Beaufort House in Copse Road, a nice bit of recycling.

A CLOSER LOOK AT THE EDGARLEY, at the time when it was being demolished.

JAMES COTTLE built the house on the right, Stancliffe, in 1841, and the next one, Melbourne, some years afterwards. His descendants still own these houses now. He quarried the rock from a site to the right of Stancliffe, causing great complaint about flying masonry narrowly missing worthy townsfolk.

AFTER THE ROYAL HOTEL AND THE YORK HOTEL CLOSED in Hill Road, there was much concern locally about the lack of a large boarding establishment. So the Walton Park Hotel Company was formed, and subscriptions raised to build our largest hotel even now.

THE CLUTTERED, FUSSY COMFORT of the interiors of Victorian apartments is apparent in this photograph. This is what the sitting room was like in No. 2 Leagrove Road in 1895.

SECTION FIVE

Village Shops: The Triangle

THERE WERE THREE LARGE TREES IN THE TRIANGLE when the fountain now moved to the end of Victoria Road was erected there in 1867. This photograph shows Alfred Coles' tailoring shop, on this site from about 1867 to 1871. The main attraction, though, is the shop belonging to William Pinkham Gannicliff and his wife, Ann. The family continued in the shop for well over 100 years, making it the longest-established business in the town.

WHEN A ROYAL CELEBRATION OF ANY SORT WAS IN ORDER, shopkeepers really went to town, the argument being that not only existing customers, but potential customers would notice your patriotic display and flock to the shop to buy. This is Gannicliffts again, at the time, I think, of the coronation of George V and Queen Mary.

WHEN THE MIDLAND BANK REBUILT on the site of this shop they got it right. In 1910, when Mr Tinklin had his creamery here, this was No. 1 Solva Place. The Tinklins were farmers, like most Clevedon dairymen.

TO THE RIGHT OF THIS PAIR OF SHOPS is the Railway Arms, since renamed the Clock Tower. It is now the Triangle branch of the Halifax Building Society. At various times these shops have been a boot-maker's and a fried fish shop – quite a contrast.

MR EDWARDS' CORN STORES, now engulfed by the Triangle Club, was at No. 3 Old Church Road. He moved into the newly-built premises in 1872, and the family ran the shop there until about 1925.

MR GOULD'S SHOP, with his name in stained glass which is still there. A display of meat like this, though, is seldom seen now, and neither is such magnificent gas lighting.

MR GEORGE GOULD HIMSELF, with an extremely smart turnout. Note the polished hoofs. His shop is now run by Jim Marsh on the corner of the Triangle.

W.E. LLOYD'S BARBERS SHOP at No. 10b The Triangle in 1906. Believe it or not, this is now part of W.H. Smith's.

F. TAYLOR, FRUITERER, in the shop now called 'Greetings'. He moved here around 1914, when this row of shops, called Moat Buildings, had been established for about twenty years. They were built next to Moat House, hence the name.

MOAT HOUSE was built by James Cottle during the late 1830s, and was run for many years by G.C. Turner as an ironmongery. His display technique was very geometrical; the little row of stone hot water bottles on the pavement looks almost like a toy train at first glance. Before it was replaced by Woolworth's, this was one of Old Street's earlier shops.

BILLETT'S adjoined the former Co-op in Old Church Road, which has now been divided, making a small shopping mall. Selling flowers and fruit, Mr Billett was bound to deal in the famous Clevedon Violets, bred by George Lee in his nurseries at Tickenham. It was said that the railway station was saturated with the strong scent of these flowers, which were sent all over the country.

OLD CHURCH ROAD, with Kiddle in Salisbury House. Just beyond Kiddle's, with the projecting sign, is O.J. House, maker of boots and shoes. This is the Garden Shop now, but the central door, caught in the right light, still shows remains of the engraving of Mr House's advert of the turn of the century.

SECTION SIX

Village Shops: East Clevedon and Old Street

A DELIVERY OF LYON'S CAKES at the Bristol House, East Clevedon Triangle, c. 1960. Hale's Cakes were just over the road! Intruding on the left of the picture is the tree which formerly stood in the centre of the Triangle. At one time there was a seat under it, and a drinking trough.

STONEBRIDGE HOUSE after Mr Griffin had moved into it from the shop on the corner of Griffin Road and Kenn Road. He took over from Rawlings and Isgar, who also described themselves as family grocers. It is now a hairdresser's shop at East Clevedon Triangle.

YEATES were also coal merchants, as their advertisements said in 1926, when they supplied the best household coal at special prices for truck loads. They are still in the same two trades, at the same address.

THE SHOP-FRONT HAS GONE from No. 169 Old Street now, where H. Parsons had a baker and confectioner's shop. He also provided teas, ices and minerals as there were more pedestrians in Old Street in those days.

THIS COTTAGE stood by the Salvation Army Hall in Old Street. It was the farmhouse for a small-holding run by Thomas Hollyman in the eighteenth century.

THE MOTORBIKE IS A DUNELT, originally made in 1925/6, and displayed here by Arthur Denmead. This had been a cycle shop, run by Willcocks, in 1902. He moved in 1914 and a grocer took over, then it became a cycle shop again.

THE CORN STORES IN OLD STREET in 1975, now Alexander Furnishings. The shop-front dates back to about 1845, when Edmund Candy set up his grocery shop here.

FRED GAGE'S OLD SIGNBOARD turned up during Chappell and Matthews' alterations to Bill Bryant's old premises in the Triangle. Fred Gage was here in 1926, making breeches, selling hats, socks, Radiac shirts and Two Steeples underwear, and charging Bristol prices.

MR ROBERTSON OUTSIDE HIS ELECTRICAL SHOP at the bottom of Chapel Hill. This is a hairdressing shop now.

SECTION SEVEN

Village Shops: The Fringes

MR EYRES, next to the Baptist chapel in Station Road, was not only a baker and confectioner, but served tea and refreshments. He delivered bread daily to all parts of town, too.

MR EYRES OF STATION ROAD, with his trap for bread deliveries, behind Moat Buildings in Old Street, where he used some of the stabling belonging to the Cottle family.

GEORGE HANCOCK was a rival to the *Mercury* at one time, printing a second local newspaper for a few years in the late '20s. He also produced a local street directory and, as you can see from the window display, a lot of posters.

THE STATION ROAD DAIRY. The brass churn in the right-hand window was a beauty. I often wonder where it ended up when the shop closed ten or fifteen years ago.

THE OLD BRITANNIA STORES on the corner of Moor Lane and Kenn Road, run by A.G. Binding and Son. It was demolished to make way for better motorway access. The signwriter is pictured below.

MR HOLLYMAN, THE SIGNWRITER. A family occupation, in a way, when you consider that at least three of his forebears had been house painters.

TOM AND MARIANNE LILLY standing outside the shop their father bought from Mr Westcott in Kenn Road in 1914. They knew everyone in the road, and far beyond, to the limits of the oil and delivery round that went with the shop. The row of houses has gone now, and there are flats for the elderly on the site, just by the garage. The river ran along the right-hand side of the shop, and the children used to paddle along it in a tin tub.

AT THE BOTTOM OF QUEEN'S ROAD, this is one of several ventures set up by the resourceful Mr Willcocks, who ran West End Garage for many years.

ALL SORTS OF TRADES were carried on in Clevedon. In Parnell Road, at No. 10a, you could buy second-hand clothes, which we call 'as new' nowadays, from Mrs Hurley.

THE CARVED STONE PANELS are still a delight on this building now that its a branch of Spar at the west end of Old Church Road. Mr Cox certainly showed his skills. J.N. Cox's son, Victor, built the cinema.

SECTION EIGHT

Shopping on The Hill

WESTCOMBE'S GROCERY on the left of Hill Road here is now Murray's Bistro and Granby Antiques. The Clevedon Bazaar, now Shore's shoe shop is next door, followed by Oram's Creamery. Melrose Cottage's front garden comes next. The house was used by Mr Hazell, the photographer, and Mr Dew, a dentist, and only later was the present shop built over the garden itself. Mr Perkins had both Studio 2 and Floyd's. On the opposite side we have Mr Yard's general and fancy draper's shop, after which comes the garden, which the saddler's shop stands on now.

THE FIRST TRAVEL AGENT'S IN CLEVEDON, at 67 Hill Road. The business was set up in the fifties; it would be nice to believe that, until then, no-one needed to go on holiday from Clevedon.

THIS WONDERFUL DISPLAY was made by Mr Brett, fishmonger, poulterer and licensed dealer in game of 3 Regent Place, in Hill Road. Families were waited on daily with a price list; the telephone number in 1912 was 55X. It is now a hairdresser's.

MR FREDERICK HORDLE outside his Hill Road shop. His sons took over the business after his death, and many Clevedonians still remember the shop being emptied of iron hoops, tin baths and other Victorian delights after they, too, had passed away and the shop was sold.

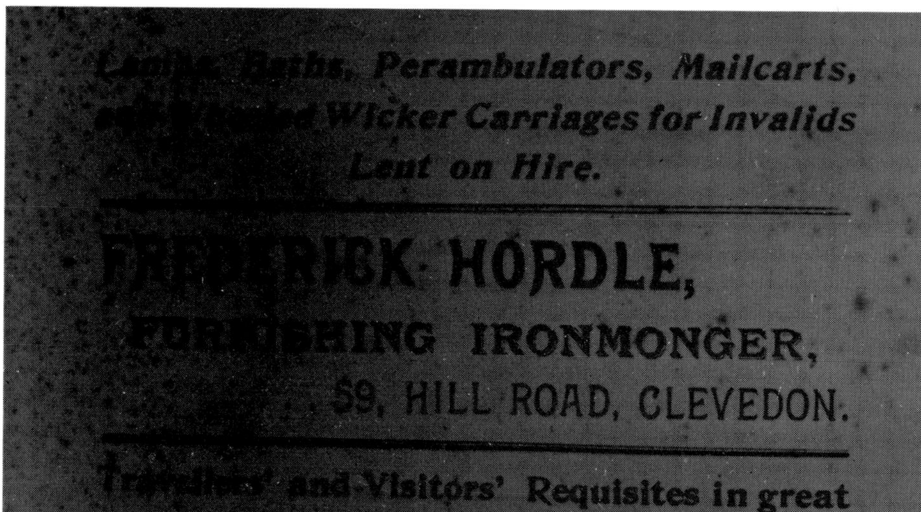

MR HORDLE'S TRADE CARD, giving extensive details of his stock and services. Neale's shop is on the site now.

SEELEY'S have not always been in their present shop. In 1903 they were where the bakery is now, hiring out pianos and dealing in stationery and fancy goods.

A RATHER BLURRED EARLY PICTURE OF HILL ROAD. The front of Caterpillars, to the right behind the lamp post, shows its old stone surround. Most exciting, just beyond the horse's head is Mr Lee's modest conservatory frontage on Warwick House, now Seeley's shop. Hagley's had half the premises from 1861 till they moved opposite into Selwood House. His daughter ran the shop until the early twenties. He established and grew the Clevedon Violets and sold home-grown fruit, flowers and vegetables.

THE OLD POST OFFICE, Rockleaze, in Hill Road, decorated for the coronation of George V in 1910.

CHALLICOM'S SHOP IN HILL ROAD, before the new extension was built to the left. They were the agents for 'Zorst' vaccuum cleaners and hired out perambulators and Bath chairs.

PARKER'S STORES in Handel House, Hill Road, shown here in 1912. Mr J.B. Parker had been the head of the business for sixteen years by then, with a total of forty years experience in the grocery trade. It is still a foodstore now.

THE INTERIOR OF THE GROCERY DEPARTMENT of Parker's Stores, a beautiful example of what the inside of a proper shop should be: all stock stacked neatly to the roof, and a comfortable bentwood chair for the customers.

SELWOOD HOUSE was built in Hill Road for Edward Hagley in 1868, when he moved across the road from Warwick House. From the footpath leading down into Gardens Road, look up at the back windows, where you can see engraved glass advertising the talents of the owner.

ALFRED WICKENDEN ran the Regent in Hill Road as a baker and confectioner for about thirty years, from 1880 until 1910. He catered for balls, wedding breakfasts, at homes and all social functions, also hiring out a large hall for dancing and parties.

MARKS THE CHEMIST, Marine House, Hill Road, with the royal coat of arms proudly displayed. The shop has been a chemist's since it was built, beginning with Mr Ransford, who sold camphor julep, scouring drops, stationery, wine, marking ink and glue. He also ran a circulating library. A visit to the shop to see the interior is a worthwhile expedition.

MR CHARLES CAPLE'S PACIFIC STORES at the top of Alexandra Road sold fine Mysore coffee at 1s. 8d. per pound along with an amazing range of other things. They obviously trusted dogs with their cheese in those days, leaving ten fine truckles out on the pavement for display!

THE CO-OPERATIVE DAIRY had taken over this shop in Alexandra Road from Ernest Dyer's Kenn Court Dairy when this photograph was taken. Next door has always been a butcher's shop, but this one has changed from furniture to dairying to restaurant, china shop, computer showrooms, and now sells silk flowers.

MR RUSSELL'S SHOP used to be in Alexandra Road, between the Reading House and St Peter's church. Clevedon's first public library began here, run by a team of volunteers. In 1926 his advertisement mentions fancy goods, an extensive art department, picture-framing, and development and enlargement of photographic films. Perhaps some of the pictures I have used here first saw the light of day in his shop.

JAMES HODDELL'S OFFICES were on this corner of Gardens Road and Alexandra Road at the turn of the century. He was the oldest established estate agent in the district.

THE TEA EXCHANGE AND BASKET EMPORIUM, established just after the First World War, an unusual mixture of businesses. This is now Indigo in Alexandra Road. They do not sell tea, but you can still get basketware there.

THIS PLOT AT SIXWAYS was purchased by the Clevedon Printing Company on 31 December 1894 for office development. They employed William Albert Green as the builder, and here are his workmen. Nowadays you could say that it would not be difficult to catch everyone on a building site standing still, or even sitting on a wall. In those days, of course, it was an extremely rare occurrence; they *had* to stand still for the photographer, however unwillingly! Barclays Bank stands here nowadays.

THIS HANDSOME CHARABANC was in use here for the workers employed by Mr William Hill, the local builder. He is standing to the right.

SECTION NINE

A Handful of Farms

HIGHDALE FARM, with the old dairy thatched. The farm dates back in written records to 1297, but the house has been rebuilt several times since that date. This picture is about 600 years more recent than that.

MASKELL'S FARM, converted for use as St John's School until the present buildings were put up. The building dated back to the late sixteenth century in the hands of the Maskell family. When their lease lapsed, it was taken over by Roger Stone, who eventually owned nine leases in the Manor of Clevedon. He had a reputation as a bit of a rustler.

THE RICKYARD OF TUTTON FARM, with William Chinn and Fred James helping to build and thatch hayricks. The picture was taken in 1894, when Charlie Wallis was there, as you can see from his name on the wain. All the stages of haymaking are shown here: the old chap with the horse-drawn mower stands in front of the next wain of mown hay; behind the girl feeding his horse is a horse-drawn rake, as well as the wooden rakes for the final tidying up of the yard.

THE OLDEST PART OF THE FARM is between the two middle chimneys.

TUTTON FARM just before it was knocked down in 1976. The house had been rebuilt around a medieval doorway in the mid-seventeenth century. It was named after John Tutton of Wrington, who leased it in 1731.

WEST END FARM, NOW TENNYSON HOUSE, long before the building of St Andrew's Drive, or the bungalows now opposite the house. This is a better view of the front than you can see now; there are too many trees in the garden.

LEGEND HAS IT, wrongly, that Tennyson stayed here when he visited the grave of his friend Arthur Hallam at St Andrew's during his honeymoon tour. In fact, the name started when the house, originally a farm, became a guest house in the thirties. It is now one of only two thatched houses in Clevedon, and was built in the early seventeenth century by a family called Burryatt.

WALTON ST MARY, before its incorporation into Clevedon in the late twenties. This is taken from behind Old Park House, the oldest building in this area, the seventeenth-century warren lodge for the rabbit park which covered 200 acres of the Hill.

OLD PARK HOUSE was the only house shown in this part of Clevedon in 1839. Until methods of gathering rainwater for household use improved, it remained so, as the limestone of this area retains no surface water.

SECTION TEN

Sport

THE BOWLING CLUB IN PRINCES ROAD opened in the early 1900s. This tiny pavilion, much expanded, is still there today.

THE NEXT STAGE in the Bowling Club's development of their pavilion was to extend to the left of the older building. The trees outside the shop at the bottom of Park Road are long gone.

AN OUTING THE BOWLING CLUB TOOK TO THE SOUTH COAST about eighty years ago. The gentleman third from left in the front row is W.J.C. Bryant, the grandfather of David Bryant, Clevedon's world champion bowler.

THE GAME OF PUSH-BALL seems to have died out now, although it was played on the Salthouse Fields in 1929. This match was sponsored by the *Daily Mail*.

A STURDY-LOOKING CLEVEDON FOOTBALL CLUB. This is the sister print to the All Saints' choir picture on page 118, dating also from the early part of this century. The shirts are nicely standardized, but not, you will notice, the socks.

AN UNDATED PHOTOGRAPH OF AN OLD WALTON FOOTBALL TEAM, taken I imagine during the thirties. Back row, left to right: Mr Reed, W. Newton, Jim Hurdle, Reg Brooks, S. James, Revd Barker. Middle row: Arthur Davies, Frank Murley, Sam Harris. Front row: Reg Youde, Les Leigh, George Bees(?), Len Maxton, Terry Banwell.

THE RIFLE CLUB out on a shoot in 1907. The photographer must have had nerves of steel.

WARTIME FIREARMS PRACTICE down at the old rifle butts on the sea-wall. This was where the Rifle Club held their meetings.

THIS WAS TAKEN at the back of Old Park Farm in Old Park Road, during Cricket Week, 1882. The Stock family came to stay in Clevedon regularly, and loved to go walking and picnicking.

AN AMATEUR CRICKET TEAM in 1929 on 'Yeates Pitch', as the field where Hillview Avenue stands was nicknamed. The boys are, back row, left to right: Bert Lilly, Tom Baker; front row: Reg Brice, Harry Lilly, Tom Hollier.

A PART OF CLEVEDON that really seems to be a quiet little backwater: the old sheds down at the Pill, used by the Sailing Club.

CLEVEDON HAS OFTEN BEEN VISITED BY THE FAMOUS, including Lady Baden-Powell, seen in 1919 outside Firwood in Highdale Road with Miss Agnes Elton. The girls of the GFS 8th company were, left to right, Ellen Hayes, Winnie Seeley, Beatrice Palmer, Gladys Lawrence, Mrs Staveley (the examiner for the British Legion), Miss Agnes Elton, Lady Baden-Powell, Miss Malcolm (District Commissioner), Janet Curtis (back), Phyllis Bray, Eva Tripp (top of head), Nora Walter, Edith Walter, Joan Parker, Beatrice Smith, Margery Sims (back row) and Joyce Seeley.

THE MARINE LAKE IN ITS HEYDAY. When the lake opened, on 30 March 1929, it was years in advance of the facilities for swimming at any other resort on the North Somerset coast. Nowadays, the sea water which fills it is filthy. Paradoxically, many people blame the lake for this!

FISHERMEN ON THE PIER. The old gas lamps were still there a relatively short time ago.

SECTION ELEVEN

Relaxation

THE SILVER BAND IN 1912, the bandstand itself still with its old lighting and the windshields needed for the band to be heard over a Clevedon summer. Back row, left to right: J. Ware, P. Hand, ? Hobbs, ? Godwin. Middle row: A. Ware, T. Godwin, W. Gliddon, S. Hole, -?-, F. Ware (bandmaster), A.O. Tanner, -?-, B. Knight, A. Ware, H. Stacey, S. Davis. Front row: E. Fry, F. Wyatt, L. Reed, F. Seckington (treasurer), T. Hole (chairman), G. Hoye, F. Rossiter, A. Brookes.

THE GLASS PAVILION was replaced in recent years by the coastguard station. When it was built, it was the bee's knees for indoor dancing and entertainment.

A GREAT ATTRACTION, arranged by Willcocks West End Garage, down by Salthouse Fields.

THIS FINE G.N. IVATT-ATLANTIC $9\frac{1}{2}$ IN GAUGE MINIATURE ENGINE ran on the line around Salthouse Fields some thirty years ago. The driver sat on the tender, not coupled up in the picture. The contraption on the funnel was to help in firing.

MR HARRY STOCK, outside the Skating Rink in Linden Road in 1892. The rink's interior is shown in the photograph of the Dairy School on page 152. Standing opposite the bottom of Herbert Road, it was built in the 1870s when the craze for roller-skating took off. The Lawn Tennis and Archery Club nearby offered other distractions.

A BUNCH OF CHAPS OUT FOR A SWIM in the river down on the sea-wall in the later twenties. This was for the experienced swimmers. Youngsters would swim in the Land Yeo below the Court where it crossed Court Lane. There was a good stretch of safe shallows there.

SHELLEY AVENUE has been built all over this idyllic picnic spot. The back of Moor Lane is in the distance, with the gasholders and abattoir, otherwise it is just open country with a few farmhouses. Left to right: Joan Bird, Phyllis Ford, Sybil Bowman, Betty Lilly, Tom Hale, Doris Plumley and Bobby, Bert Parsons, Bob Hasnip, Harry Lilly and Bert Lilly. This was taken sixty years ago.

THE GENTLEMAN with the rolled-up sack under one arm is Sammy Hamlin, the proud exhibitor of this swordfish, washed up on shore here in the twenties. He showed it for quite a while, taking it round the pubs in a wheelbarrow, until he was found sitting outside one of the town's hostelries saying, 'It *don't* stink.'

SOME OF THE MEN FROM KENN ROAD having a quiet card game in the late twenties. If, and I stress the if, any stakes were put down, they were put in someone's cap. Then, if the game was disturbed, the cap could be whipped back on, and the money hidden.

SECTION TWELVE

The Carnivals and the Picture House

'KINDLY HELP OUR COTTAGE HOSPITAL', reads the slogan above Tommy and Daisy Durbin's shop window in Old Street. They ran a sweet shop there for many years.

THIS WAS TAKEN from the balcony of the Wagon and Horses in about 1930, and shows Frank Knight's old cottage and fish and chip shop very well.

ONE OF THE PRE-WAR CARNIVALS passing along Old Church Road. At the bottom of Marson Road Mr Clement still had his saddlery. The triangular sign projecting from the shop next door belonged to Mr Hole, the fruiterer.

THE CHILDREN IN KENN ROAD decided to have their own carnival in the early thirties, and this is the result. These are children from the Powell, Brice, Brooks, Chard and Short families, with their friends.

THE SILVER BAND used to practice in the brick building behind them in Tickenham Road during the thirties. This must be one of the carnivals getting ready for 'take-off' around this time.

CARNIVAL FLOATS GATHERING IN WALTON ROAD before the war could encounter the 'Mayor and Mayoress' of Clevedon, alias Hedley Long and Frank Maynard, driven by Mr Drewett.

IN THE CARNIVAL PROCESSION of 1935, Donald Long took to his bed – the best decorated bicycle I have seen.

MR NORMAN BAKER, OF WRANGLE FARM, AND DAISY DURBIN as Pearly King and Queen.

MR COX'S FIRST CINEMA constructed in 1912, 40 ft long and 27 ft wide, now underneath the west end of the present building. This seated 200 people and had a sliding roof. After eighteen months, it was enlarged to seat 389, without missing one night's film show.

THIS WAS TAKEN during the last stages of building the new cinema, constructed horizontally over the old one, between 1920 and 1922, again without missing one filmshow.

OUR PRESENT CURZON used not only to have two box offices; it had a porter-cum-commissionaire. He holds one of the programmes which were then produced by every cinema for its shows. Unfortunately, the only thing readable on it is 'Picture House', the name of the cinema until 1945 when it changed to the Maxine.

THE INTERIOR OF THE CURZON has not been this grandiose for some years now. I remember sitting in the balcony, but the boxes went long before my time. The organ, built by Percy Daniel Organ Works at East Clevedon, can be seen in the box to the right of the stage. Mr Cox played this himself, and his stepmother, Blanche Harwood, a famous stage singer of the day, entertained the audience during the intervals. The outside of the building can be seen on the screen.

ABOVE THE CURZON in the twenties and thirties, you could treat yourself to a light tea in the Oak Room Café before the nightly showings. Now run as a picture gallery, it is little changed. At the end of the café furthest from the photographer was the foyer, complete with piano and easy chairs.

UPSTAIRS IN THE PICTURE HOUSE. This detail of the foyer shows the stained glass in the distinctive semicircular windows of the foyer. The sculpture was probably the work of Mr Victor Cox, who built the old cinema in 1912, rebuilding it in its present form in 1920–22. He was a monumental mason, the son of J.N. Cox, whose premises at the West End of Clevedon appear on page 68.

SECTION THIRTEEN

Schools

NOW OFFICES, AND WITHOUT ITS SPIRE, this school has changed relatively little on the outside since 1858 when rebuilding took place on the site of the first school, constructed here in 1834. Until the Infant School opened in 1846, it was the only free school in Clevedon.

ST ANDREW'S BOYS in the early twenties. From top left to bottom right: Herbert Bolt, George Horsey, Stan James, Charlie Paynter, Ernie Youde, Jack Clark, Clifford Moxham, Jim Radnor, Alfie Hollyman, Fred Bray, Fred Cheesewright, Fred Janes, Horace Hatch, George Bees, Leonard Head, Charlie Dimond, Harold Abrams, Sid Fortune, Arthur Hampton, 'Jumbo' Ellis, Eddie Aldom, Sammy Amos, Jack Rollings, Ron Smith, Bob Goodliffe, Tom Lilly, Fred Cook, Arthur Smart, Monty Feltham, Les Burge, Jack Binding, Tom Binding.

THE GIRLS AT ST ANDREW'S in the early twenties. Top left to bottom right: Gladys Fry, Birdie Hill, Frances King, Winnie Dors, Margery Elston, Marianne Lilly, Doris Moxham, Joan Gibson, Emily Hurley, Vera Davies, Rose Fortune, Kitty Palmer, Winnie Blake, Gladys Parsons, Constance Carey, Edith Hampton, -?-.

ST ANDREW'S INFANTS in 1920. Top left to bottom right: Ken Hack, Harry Lilly, Rose Wilkins, Elsie Hill, -?-, Mona Gibson, Les Cox(?), Ron Hack, Ray Mogg, Sid Ball, -?-, Hetty Short, Joan Palmer, Kathleen Rogers, Kathleen Crease, Lily Wilkins, -?-, Bert Lilly, Charlie Rhodes, Frank Webb, Fred Chard, Percy Pople, -?-, -?-, -?-, -?-, Graham Godding.

ST LEONARD'S SCHOOL was run by Mr James Usher, in the middle row with the white hair. His son, Gray Usher, who for so many years wrote the 'Spade and Plough' column in the *Clevedon Mercury*, is on his right. George Jarrett is second from right in the back row. The school was in Madeira Road.

THE GIRLS OF MISS DUNFORD'S ACADEMY, at Wycliffe, in Linden Road, ready to perform their Christmas play. Some of these girls may have been the ones who danced at the Old English Fair held at Clevedon Court in 1912, when Miss Dunford's pupils danced Pop goes the Weasel, Jenny pluck Pears, The Jolly Miller and other country dances.

SECTION FOURTEEN

Church and Chapel

THE CEREMONY OF LAYING THE FIRST STONE for the Baptist Men's Own Hall in Station Road, in 1903.

THE HALL ON COMPLETION. The road in front is still not made up, the hall being on the end of the first row of buildings in Station Road.

AN OUTING FOR THE WESLEYAN METHODISTS, pulled by Shopland's traction engine in the early part of this century. The chapel was designed by Mr Herbert J. Jones, architect, and built in 1883. The tree in the left foreground is now fully mature, and has long outgrown its railings.

ELLA BLACKWELL, an old Clevedonian, wrote to me nine years ago, 'All Saints'. . . had a very good choir and the organist and choir master was Percy Daniel. They also had a small orchestra, Mr Arthur Tanner played the violin, Mr Gannicliffy the cornet and my father John Grey the cello.' Ella was then in her eighties, speaking of the time before the First World War when she was young.

THE CEREMONY OF BLESSING THE PLOUGH, carried out here by the vicar of All Saints' in 1935.

ST ANDREW'S CHOIR, Easter Sunday 1928. Many of these well-scrubbed youngsters were later members of the Excelsior Club. Back row, left to right: Sonny Hack, Ron Hack, Graham Godding, Ray Mogg, Edward Youde, Jack Bishop, Harry Lilly. Front row: Tom Hollier, Mervyn Hack, Bert Lilly, Sid Ball, Donald Baker, Joseph Baker, Norman Ford.

THE MEMBERS OF THE EXCELSIOR CLUB in the early thirties. This is in Highdale Avenue; it is now the bicycle shop. Those who attended St Andrew's church met here for skittles and other activities. My father, Bert Lilly, is seventh from the left in the back row. The president was the vicar of Clevedon, preb. Badcock, and the steward was Mr W. Hack, who lived in the house.

THIS ENTERTAINMENT took place in the gardens of All Saints' Vicarage just before the First World War, and was performed by the pupils of All Saints' School, now officially called East Clevedon Junior School.

THE CAST OF *SLEEPING BEAUTY*, when it was performed by the school in All Saints' Hall in Old Street some seventy-odd years ago. The hall was completed in 1913.

SECTION FIFTEEN

Serving the People

BOTH OF THESE BUILDINGS have seen a change of use since this photograph was taken. The church is now part of a complex of apartments. The old post office, Rockleaze, has been a Labour Exchange and is now offices. In 1898 Frederick Hodder took a contract to fetch the mail from the railway station, seven trips down and five trips up daily, to be pulled by one horse driven by a sober respectable driver not less than eighteen years of age. The mailcart is probably the one he used.

THE ENTIRE STAFF OF THE CLEVEDON POST OFFICE a few years after 1900. Imagine being served by the ladies with their beautiful hats. The gentleman standing on the extreme right is George Jarrett's father.

THE OLD POLICE STATION used to stand where Great Western Way joins Old Church Road. It replaced the first police station, at Nos 17 and 18 Chapel Hill, in 1888, and was itself replaced in the sixties by the current one in Queen's Road.

THE INSCRIPTION OVER THE DOOR, exposed during alterations fifteen years ago.

THE FIRE BRIGADE in August 1922, called out to a hayrick fire on Sir Charles Miles' property.

YOU CAN SEE WHY they bought the Leyland two years later. Also taken in August 1922.

THE FIRE BRIGADE in the days before they moved across Old Street from this shed to their present HQ. The old engine was drawn by the council's horses, which usually pulled the refuse cart. When the steam hooter at the gasworks was sounded, these horses could be seen careering through the town on their way to Old Street, sometimes without the driver!

TEDDY DAWES, putting Clevedon's old fire-engine up for sale at Yatton Market in 1924, when it was replaced by a solid-tyred Leyland.

A PROUD MEMBER OF THE CLEVEDON FIRE BRIGADE, showing off the Leyland bought in 1924, one of the succession of fire-engines they have used since they were formed in 1883.

THE FUNERAL PROCESSION OF SIR EDMUND ELTON leaving the gates of Clevedon Court on 28 July 1920. The horse-drawn fire-engine was used as a hearse, pulled by the men of the fire brigade set up by Sir Edmund's efforts in 1883. The silver helmet he wore as Captain can be seen on top of the coffin.

THE FIRST SOMERSET ARTILLERY VOLUNTEERS. This may have been taken at their Drill Hall in Albert Road, or at the magazine and heavy-gun range on Wains Hill, about Battery Cottages. They also had a carbine range near Gull House on the sea-wall. Membership in 1897 stood at eighty, with Lieutenant-Colonel Sir Edmund Elton, Bt., Captain A.B. Trestrail, Lieutenant H. Coates, 2nd Lieutenant A.E.Y. Trestrail, Sergeant-Major Hood, Quartermaster-Sergeant T. Binding, Sergeants F. Blackmore and W. Hack, Corporals J. Blackmore and C. Clarke. This picture is undated.

THIS PHOTOGRAPH OF THE 7TH KING'S OWN LANCE REGIMENT marching off to war was taken in 1915, with the crossing gates of the Weston, Clevedon and Portishead Light Railway showing clearly in the foreground and to the right. The men were to travel on the Great Western line, however.

THE SOUTH CLEVEDON BATTALION OF THE HOME GUARD, commanded by William Hand, sixth from left in the front row. There are, as you can see, some forces' ex-members on leave who have been included in the back row. Their HQ was the skittle alley at the gasworks in Moor Lane.

ANOTHER OF CLEVEDON'S HOME GUARD BATTALIONS. Fifth from right in the bottom row is George Jarrett, a well-liked local character and writer on agricultural matters. A booklet he possessed about the setting up of the Home Guard locally said that in practice manoeuvres, the men aged around 45 had the most staying power. There is hope yet for the middle-aged.

THIS PART OF THE COTTAGE HOSPITAL, opened in 1875, used to be a barn in the lower farmyard of Highdale Farm. The dispensary, designed by Hans Price, opened ten years earlier, and must have given health care a very open-air, farm-like appearance.

JACKO BREWER was well known in Clevedon for many years. Like many people, he was horrified to learn from cinema newsreels that there were often no ambulances available to take wounded soldiers from the battlefields during the First World War, and his reaction was to set to and raise enough money to buy this one.

A MAGNIFICENT STEAMROLLER, owned by the Local Board of Health, which became the Urban District Council in 1894. It is seen here in Wellington Terrace, which was then in Walton St Mary.

THE LAST STEAMROLLER owned by the Urban District Council, in action along the Beach in the mid-sixties. This must have been taken when all the children were in school. When I used to rush out to watch it, there was always a crowd in the way.

SECTION SIXTEEN

Travelling About

THE SMITHY IN OLD STREET which used to stand in front of the Health Centre site. It was run by M.W. Harris.

THE SMITHY IN WALTON ROAD run by Sam Harris. The Light Railway crossed by the smithy, and Mr Harris was supposed to open the gates for the train when it whistled. In practice, he was very deaf, and usually an eager lad ended up doing it for him.

WEST END MOTORS, set up by Mr Willcocks. An advertisement of 1926 shows the place looking like this, with a very attractive deco-style frontage. This was taken just three years after, and shows the way it would have been seen from Salthouse Fields.

RICHARD STEPHENS' CARS arrayed beneath the Triangle Clock for this advertising photograph taken in 1903.

MR RICHARD STEPHENS, driving with his family in one of the cars he built in his workshops in the Triangle. On the back seat is his son, R.J. Stephens, who in 1962 still owned one of his father's cars, built in 1898. He wrote of the trial runs that, 'tube ignition was used, the burners being under the driver's seat, and although precautions were taken some little excitement was caused when it was discovered the seat was on fire and had to be hastily removed and rubbed on the grass verge to put it out.' The site of the Engineering Works belonging to Mr Stephens is now occupied by the carpet shop near the Conservative Club.

TRANSPORT WAS QUICKER BY SEA before the First World War, and here at Clevedon Pill boats used to come from Wales and South Somerset to unload.

SECTION SEVENTEEN

Catching the Train

THE SIDE OF THE GREAT WESTERN STATION you could see from Kenn Road, fronting on to the yard. The original station building was of timber.

THE REST OF THE STATION FRONT, facing down Kenn Road. Before the station was demolished, the town's Christmas tree used to stand by the side of the building nearest the Triangle.

MR AND MRS YOUDE, from Strode Road, collecting some visitors from the station.

THIS USED TO HAPPEN! The train had pushed its carriages right through the back of the old timber-built station and out into the street in 1884. We are looking north; beyond the train, Smith's had not been built. The boy in the centre foreground has a very 'Told you so' look about him.

DEFINITELY THE END OF THE LINE for the Great Western station. You can see the old front, beyond the buffers, which the old trains used to go through occasionally. This happened one day when Bill Hill's father was crossing the road and found the train ploughing its way towards him!

THE CAR PARK SIDE OF THE STATION. The gates were still *in situ* when the site was finally developed in 1986/7.

THE OLD SIGNAL BOX for the Great Western at Clevedon, which stood on the platform, a little beyond the goods shed.

THE GREAT WESTERN GOODS SHED being dismantled tile by tile in 1969. Behind it on the left is the part of Melbourne Terrace which used to be called Railway View.

THE WESTON, CLEVEDON AND PORTISHEAD LIGHT RAILWAY TRAINS came out from the side of the Conservative Club, crossed the road, and went over in front of Smith's. Small boys waited till the lever released the crossing gates and then ran out and leapt on for a swing across the road. Frank Knight waits to cross with his sack trucks.

SECTION EIGHTEEN

Hard Work

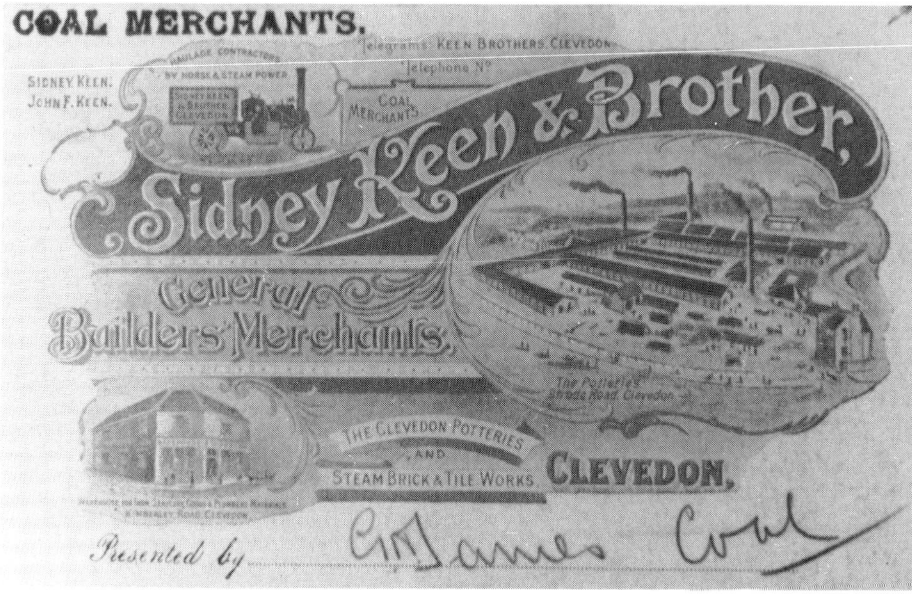

A PICTORIAL TRADE CARD, showing the Potteries at Strode Road and the warehouse for sanitary goods and plumber's materials in Kimberley Road. Colonel Sidney Keen's works were the largest in the town and many of the roof tiles of Clevedon still bear his stamp.

THE *BESSIE* FROM BARNSTAPLE, anchored at Clevedon Pill some seventy-odd years ago. Coal boats also used to call here, delivering for the brickworks in Strode Road and Kenn Road.

THE KENN ROAD POTTERY, run by Mr Charles H. Lewis and Mr Rolling, here standing in the centre. Plain and decorative pots, as well as small household items, were produced here. When the pottery closed just before the First World War, the potter went to work for Colonel Keen at the Strode Road brickworks. The pottery was to the rear of No. 34 Kenn Road. The next row of houses down has some excellent tiles, produced here, on its bay windows.

THE PUGGING MILL, which worked grit out of the clay, run by a donkey.

THE RANGE PRODUCED BY THE POTTERY IN KENN ROAD, easily datable to the early part of this century by the portrait busts of Kitchener. Some of these pots can still be seen in gardens in Clevedon now.

GEORGE MANLEY, putting handles on jugs down at the Clevedon Pottery in Court Lane sixty years ago. William Fishley Holland and George Manley had worked together at Braunton Pottery in Devon, and moved here to help Sir Ambrose Elton continue Eltonware in 1921. Holland ran his own pottery at Court Lane until his death in 1969, the business finally being sold in 1977.

SIR EDMUND ELTON AND GEORGE MASTERS are the two figures to the left, with the white pinafores, applying their Eltonware tiles and pillars to the Clock Tower. Sir Edmund presented the tower to the town to mark the Queen's Diamond Jubilee in 1897. It was completed and officially handed over the following year.

AUGUSTUS JAMES, one of the town's real old characters. His family had farmed at Bow Cottage, where Old Street Garage is now. When he was haymaking he would go into the barn opposite, now the Cottage Hospital, for a good snooze. He was the sexton at St Andrew's church for a great many years, and is reputed to have buried several vicars.

THE OLD BAKERY at the back of Fred Hale's Old Street premises. This is where, in 1929, a fire destroyed the packing room and the employees had to make an extra 2,000 Easter biscuits in a morning.

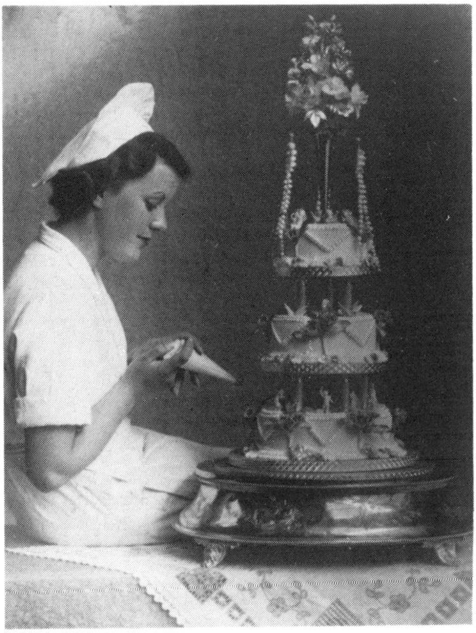

HALE'S HAD NAMES FOR THE TYPES OF CAKE you could order from their wedding and birthday cake price list. This was Audrey, here being iced by Audrey Moore. A three-tier, 15 lb cake would cost you 45s. in 1955.

SWISS ROLLS BEING MADE on the assembly line at Hale's, undated, unfortunately. The lady nearest the camera has got a lot of the factory's jam on her pinny!

THE CARNIVAL FLOAT made by Hale's workers in 1937, waiting to leave Griffin Road and join the procession. The thatched cottage was one of the firm's trade marks at the time.

HALE'S CONTRIBUTION TO THE CARNIVAL in Griffin Road, before joining the procession. The van is an Albion, and the people are, left to right: Edie Coles, Kath Hollyman, Dood Reed and Phyl Ainsworth. John Hare is looking out of the van.

CHALLICOM'S IN HILL ROAD ran a depository around 1910, employing these thoroughly reliable-looking old chaps. Left to right: G. Neath of Old Street, W. Mogridge of Copse Road, G. Clark of Kenn Road, F. Barnes of Old Street and G. Hampton of Parnell Road.

THE EMPLOYEES OF THE OLD URBAN DISTRICT COUNCIL before the Second World War. Back row, left to right: Bill Dean, Ben Colborne, Charles Coles, Ted Davis, Bill Powell, Jack Sims, Bill Morris, Edmund Shopland, Walter Davis, ? Powell, Arthur Phillpots and Bill Musto. Second row: ? Barrington, Jack Hayward, Alan Chubb, Lionel Roe, Sam Bray, Wilf Ball, George Pitts, ? Knight, ? Bryant, Paddy Hale. Front row: ? Sandy, ? Ford, George Young, ? Bray, Bill Rawlings, Ern Woodland, Lionel Mogg, ? Selwood, Fred Stone, Ted Gooding, George Tovey.

THE CLEVEDON AND PORTISHEAD STEAM LAUNDRY stood in Kimberley Road, having been established around 1905. For many years, the washing from the upper part of the town had been farmed out to the wives of local working men; some of these ladies were organized under the management of Mr Henry Stuart. I have seen more cheerful expressions on the faces of the workers, but it was a serious business having photographs taken in those days.

THE DAIRY SCHOOL, held in the old Skating Rink in Linden Road, in 1894. This occasional event was an intensive short course, held in conjunction with what was to become the Royal Bath and West Show. The teachers were Miss Williams and Miss Benjafield, their pupils here, Mrs Hardwick, Miss Stuckey, Miss Tinklin, Miss Hill, Miss Hardwick, Miss Bedall, Miss Dyer, -?-, Miss E.K. Weaver and Miss A.M. Weaver.

THE GAS PIPE GOING ACROSS THE RIVER by the Middle Yeo bridge at Kenn Road. The workmen are, left to right: Sam Genge, ? Badman, Ref Fortune, Johnny Fortune and Ted Baker.

THE CULVERTING OF THE MIDDLE YEO at Kenn Road in July 1978. The rivers round here are almost all called 'yeos'. This is the Saxon word for a river, as opposed to the Romano-British *isca*, which gives us the Exe and the Axe. Given also that, before the Conquest, Clevedon was in the hands of John the Dane, a strong foreign presence all those centuries ago might be postulated.

IMAGINE THIS LOT BEING DRIVEN PAST by the Shoplands, with a load of timber or building materials on board. In its day it was the worst you could expect in the way of traffic noise unless you lived by the railway.

E.H. HEYWOOD AT WORK cutting tree trunks with a circular saw driven off a traction engine. This was taken in Holly Lane in 1942, and looks as though it is in one of the small quarries there. Perhaps the traction engine is still about? Its number is TA1582.

SECTION NINETEEN

Occasions

THE DAMAGE SUFFERED BY THE SEA FRONT during a storm which took place around the turn of the century. The building which predated the Clevedon Sailing Club HQ can be plainly seen, as can the premises at Spray Point. Perhaps the patient line of horses and carts was waiting to take away wreckage, or delivering sandbags?

FLOODING IN KENN ROAD. This was taken in the late sixties from No. 91, and shows one of the pair of Victorian cottages opposite, since considerably extended. The water was going in through the front door and out of the back door of the cottage.

FLOODS WERE ALWAYS A PROBLEM in this part of Kenn Road. We are standing more or less on the roundabout where Great Western Way crosses, looking towards Kenn. The majority of the cottages have gone. This was taken some eighty-five years ago.

DAVID LLOYD GEORGE paying a visit to the Liberal Workingmen's Club in the Triangle. Oddly enough, the Liberal Club and the Conservative Club both opened in the same year, 1892.

LADY ELTON RE-OPENING THE PIER after the head was reconstructed at a workable angle to the tidal race in 1893.

SIR ARTHUR ELTON'S 21ST BIRTHDAY PRESENTATION in 1927. His younger brother, Ralph, is on the steps, and the gentleman making the presentation is Mr John Bishop, a worker for many years on the Court Estate.

ACKNOWLEDGEMENTS

Thanks for photographs to:

Derek Lilly • Dennis Moxham • David Long • Ray Lumbard
George Littlejones • Constance Jarrett, for the late George Jarrett
Evelyn Upton, for the late Edith Manley • Wendy Hobden • Peter Ganniclifft
Miss Billett • Bert Price • Victor Cox Clevedon Story Heritage Centre
The *Clevedon Mercury* • John Hinder • Clevedon Civic Society
Local History Group • Monica Moody.

My thanks for research facilities to Lady Elton and the Somerset Record Office.